Great Barrier Reef Adventures

Jim Cromarty

CHRISTIAN FOCUS

ISBN 1-84550-0687
Published in 2005
by
Christian Focus Publications,
Geanies House, Fearn, Tain
Ross-shire, IV20 1TW,
Great Britain

Cover design by Jonny Sherlock
Cover illustration by Graham Kennedy
Other illustrations by Fred Apps

Printed in Wales by CPD

Great Barrier Reef
Adventures

Jim Cromarty

Contents

The Great Barrier Reef

Come with me on an adventure along Australia's east coast, where you will visit many places of interest, including the only living object that can be seen from the moon - The Great Barrier Reef - (G.B.R.). Our God has created a place of absolute wonder that has been built by billions of small sea creatures called polyps. Their underwater garden is more colourful than any garden you have seen on the earth. In addition to the 400 species of polyps, there are over 2,500 categories of fish and 200 bird varieties living about the reef. Further studies tell us that there are about 400 categories of molluscs, 15 species of snakes and 500 varieties of seaweed. Just as the reef has innumerable colours, so do the creatures that live about the reef. For a moment imagine a multicoloured field of flowers of many shapes and sizes. Do you see them swaying in the breeze?

God's underwater garden is even more colourful! The small polyps have made a reef, rich in colour, which gently sways about in the tidal movements. And swimming about the coral are fish of a multitude of colours.

Many proud people spend a lot of money buying the best

and most colourful clothes, to make them stand out in the crowd. Their hope is to hear favourable comments about what they are wearing. However, the Lord has something to say about this - '... do not worry about your life, what you will eat or what you will drink; nor about your body, what you will put on .... why do you worry about clothing? Consider the lilies of the field, how they grow: They neither toil nor spin; and yet I say to you that even Solomon in all his glory was not arrayed like one of these' (Matthew 6: 25 - 29).

Australia's G.B.R stretches over two thousand kilometres along the coast of northern New South Wales and Queensland. Marine scientists tell us that in addition to the underwater reef there are more than one thousand coral islands.

As the G.B.R. wends its way through the warm waters, we read that it is between sixty and one hundred and sixty kilometres from the coastline, except at Cape Tribulation where the reef comes right to the shoreline.

Polyps, the builders of the G.B.R. are sea creatures between 2.5 cm and 2.5 m in diameter, and are usually found in colonies. They are cylindrical in shape and when released by their parent, attach one end of their body to the dead remains of other polyps. One half of their body becomes calcium and so, over the years, the reef gradually grows.

The other end of the polyp is a mouth surrounded by tentacles that wave about in the moving water searching for food - usually tiny fish. There is one polyp type that attracts a single cell algae, that buries itself in the polyp's body. It then assists the polyp make limestone and food.

I haven't the space to name the many polyps, but one is the mushroom coral. It was given this name because it looks like the underside of a mushroom. Some other coral looks like small trees, and there is brain coral, so named because its appearance is similar to the human brain. Many corals are soft while others are solid. The 'fern coral' looks lovely with its many fronds, but unlike the ferns in our gardens, it is solid!

The coral reproduction is most unusual. The polyps grow small knobs called 'buds' which are filled with eggs and sperm, ready to be released at the same moment. If you were underwater when the 'buds' burst open you would see what has been called an underwater, coloured snowstorm. This happens during either November or December, according to the time of the full moon.

The fertilised eggs float to the surface of the sea where they are moved about by wind and tide, before sinking to the ocean floor, or to the existing coral where the next generation of coral is formed.

The Australian Government has established the 'Great Barrier Reef Marine Park,' which is responsible for ensuring the reef maintains its pristine condition. When you visit the reef please take care not to damage it in any way. If you want to learn more about the reef, buy or borrow 'The Great Barrier Reef,' published in 1999 by The Australian Geographic Pty. Ltd. It has 155 pages of information about the G.B.R. There are many pictures that show the vibrant colours of the corals and fish.

The best builder of everything in the universe is God. We are plainly told that all things were created through the 'Word' who is God's Son, the Lord Jesus: 'In the beginning was the Word, and the Word was with God, and the Word was God. He was in the beginning with God. All things were made through Him, and without Him nothing was made that was made' (John 1: 1-3).

Our God is a majestic builder-God!

Australia Ahoy!

The journey to Australia, the 'Land Down Under,' was once a slow trip by ship, but today you can board an aeroplane and be there in a couple of days. Many tourists travel on QANTAS, the Australia airline - 'The Flying Kangaroo.' QANTAS is an unusual word to British speaking people because the letter 'q' is normally followed by a 'u.' However, the name QANTAS is an acronym standing for Queensland and Northern Territory Aerial Service.

QANTAS was established in 1920 at an outback town named Winton; but when the headquarters were moved to Longreach, the name of the company was changed to what we have today. Two men who played an important part in establishing QANTAS were W. Hudson Fysh and Paul McGinness. Despite just £6,850 in the company's bank account, QANTAS purchased its first aeroplane - a triplane. Because it had an open cockpit, the pilots had to wear goggles for protection against the wind, rain and dust.

A few years later, the company purchased a new plane that flew at 105 km per hour!

To help QANTAS meet all of its expenses, the company won the 1922 contract to deliver mail to the Australian outback. As well, the company delivered fresh vegetables, fish, meat, clothes, newspapers, mail and anything else that could be handled. They collected mail from the outlying areas and took it back to post offices in the larger towns.

An aeroplane was something new in the Australian outback, and with many people doubting the company would be a success, Fysh, McGinness and their workmen, including pilots, set about making the airline pay. As the planes could carry four passengers, QANTAS began a taxi service at two shillings a mile, or three guineas per passenger for a ten-minute joyride.

The first person to pay for his flight was eighty four-year-old Alexander Kennedy who loudly criticised everyone who doubted the success of the company. The company owners realised that now they could earn all the money needed to meet all expenses.

QANTAS pilots were the heroes of the outback. I read that at one Sunday school the children were asked, 'Who was Pontius Pilate?'

The reply came back very quickly, 'He's the bloke who flies the QANTAS mail plane!'

It was the Rev John Flynn who established the Flying Doctor Service. He was a Presbyterian minister who knew there were times when a doctor was urgently needed in the outback. It was a QANTAS plane that was first used to get this important scheme started.

Very early in the history of the company, QANTAS began to fly people overseas, and to do this flying boats were purchased. Now the planes could land close to the world's great cities. In 1935 a regular flight to Singapore commenced. The trip took four days! Today, the modern jets can do the trip in half a day.

During World War II QANTAS helped the Australian soldiers fighting in Papua and New Guinea by delivering much needed weapons and ammunition, and returning with injured soldiers.

After the war, the Australian Government bought many shares in QANTAS, making it truly an Australian company. Gradually the corporation expanded, buying bigger and better aircraft. In 1974 Cyclone Tracy destroyed the city of Darwin and QANTAS came to the rescue of the many people whose homes had been destroyed. People had to be quickly moved, so QANTAS on one mercy flight, carried 673 people.

Today planes travel about the world at tremendous speeds. Try to compare aeroplane travel with the Biblical characters who rode their donkeys and camels. The Lord Jesus made his last entrance into Jerusalem riding a donkey, while people shouted out, 'Hosanna to the Son of David! Blessed is He who comes in the name of the LORD! Hosanna in the highest!' (Matthew 21:9). Our Saviour didn't enter Jerusalem as a warrior seated upon a horse, but as the sacrifice for the sins of his people, soon to be abused and put to death upon a Roman cross. When Christ returns he will come as the warrior King and Judge, surrounded by his army of angels, to overthrow Satan and his followers, both demons and humans. He will at that time take his people to heaven. I pray that you are one of those joyful people who pray for Christ's return!

The next step in your adventure will commence at Melbourne, the capital city of Victoria. While in Victoria, you are going to travel along the Great Ocean Road, where you will meet The Twelve Apostles.

Meet the 12 Apostles!

You are going on just one adventure in Victoria - an adventure which is surprising in its beauty and stories of long ago. The road we will travel is the Great Ocean Road which wends its way along the rugged southern Victorian coast. It was built largely by the soldiers who returned home after World War I. Work was scarce and many men were given jobs with picks and shovels, cutting the roadway along the steep limestone cliffs. Later, during the Depression, which was a time of great unemployment and very little money, many men were given work to finish the roadway through some of Australia's most picturesque countryside.

It passes golden sand beaches, rain forests and farming areas. Along the coast there are limestone pinnacles standing tall in the ocean. Some of these cliffs are well over one hundred metres tall and bear the scars of wind and waves.

Years ago, visitors travelled along the Great Ocean Road to view 'The Sow and Piglets.' This name, given to some of the rock formations, was not very attractive and soon tourists went elsewhere. However, it was decided to change the name of the twelve towering rock formations, standing high in the ocean, and close to the shoreline to 'The Twelve Apostles'! The name caught the imagination of tourists and now many make sure they see the rocky outcrops.

It is not possible to see all twelve limestone formations from the one spot, and recently I read that there are only ten of the twelve pinnacles still standing. Strong, gale force winds and huge waves have caused the cliff faces to collapse into the ocean, to be seen no more.

When you reach Cape Ottawa, you will see a small lighthouse, about sixteen metres tall, built on a headland that is about ninety metres above sea level. This lighthouse was built in 1848 to warn ships of the rocky coastal region, where more than six hundred people had lost their lives in shipwrecks. The light can be seen twenty two miles out to sea and has proved its value in the prevention of ship wrecks and the loss of life.

In 1878 the iron hulled clipper, 'Loch Ard Gorge' hit a rocky headland with the loss of fifty four men, women and children. Only two people survived, Tom Pearce and Eva Carmichael. Tom was responsible for saving young Eva's life and later asked for her hand in marriage. She refused and returned to her relatives in Ireland. The area now carries the name of the ship that went down at that spot.

Along the Great Ocean Road is a place called 'The London Bridge.' Years ago there was a tall limestone cliff connected to a towering pinnacle out from the shore. The wind and waves had worn away the lower region leaving a 'bridge' formation between both places. The local authorities made it possible for visitors to walk across the bridge to the pinnacle out from the shore. A couple visiting the 'London Bridge' in 1990 walked across, only to see the walkway collapse into the ocean behind them, making it impossible to return to the shore without help. Later a helicopter appeared on the scene and they were rescued. I'm sure they had a great time telling their children and grandchildren of the day they almost lost their lives!

Beside the roadway, tourists will find a sign announcing the presence of a blowhole. These are places where the waves have worn caves into the limestone cliffs. Gradually the waves

force their way deeper into the cliff, and upwards until a tunnel breaks through. In days of rough weather, the waves will smash their way into the cave, forcing both air and water through the narrow tunnel and out into the open. Occasionally a monster wave fills the cave and with great force bursts out into the open air. People have lost their lives by standing too close to the opening in the rock face and being sucked into the opening as the wave recedes. That would be a terrible end to an adventure!

In the Bible we read about rocks, stones, cliff, mountains and pinnacles - 529 times in all. Many times our God is likened to a huge rock.

We are to build our lives upon this rock. Do you remember the parable of the builders? One man built his home on the sandy soil in the river bed, while the other person built his home on a rock. There was security upon the rock (Matthew 7:24-27).

The Lord Jesus is the 'ROCK' upon which we must build our life. The wind and the waves of evil cannot hurt us, as Christ, our ROCK, has all power in heaven and upon the earth. In Psalm 31:1-3. we read: ' In You, O LORD, I put my trust; Let me never be ashamed; Deliver me in Your righteousness. Bow down Your ear to me, Deliver me speedily; Be my rock of refuge, A fortress of defence to save me. For You are my rock and my fortress...' In the Saviour's day and before, people hid behind huge rocks in order to escape an enemy.

The towering limestone cliffs and pinnacles jutting upwards from the Victorian coastline are gradually being worn away, and one day all will fall. However, Christ the Rock will never fall. By trusting in him we have spiritual safety. He is the rock of my salvation! What about you?

To complete your adventure along the Great Ocean Road you should see the little fairy penguins who have a rookery near London Bridge. These small creatures are much different to their south pole cousins. Their chest is white feathered, and their back has dark blue feathers.

The fairy penguins grow to approximately 40 cm tall and weigh about a kilogram. They have a life span of about six years. The females lay two eggs in their well prepared nest, which is at the end of a 70 cm tunnel. Each year the male and female return to the same nest, which is just one in a colony of possibly several hundred birds. Both parents are responsible for feeding and caring for their youngsters.

They spend the daytime gathering food in the ocean; fish, squid, small shell fish and whatever other small juicy morsels they can find. But life in the ocean can be very dangerous for them, as they make delicious meals for sharks, seals and killer whales.

They return to the land each night, when darkness gives

them some safety from dogs, cats, foxes, eagles and other flesh eating creatures. Humans are also responsible for killing many of these little creatures. They drown when caught in fishing nets, while others become tangled in plastic bags, again drowning. Others choke on pieces of plastic, carelessly thrown into the water.

You will also find colonies of mutton birds at Port Campbell between the months of October and April. After mating and caring for their young they set out for the long flight to the Bering Sea in the cold arctic regions. Each year they fly about twenty five thousand kilometres!

Now it's back to Melbourne for a flight north to Sydney. Your adventure has only just begun!

Sydney Harbour Bridge

As your plane approaches Sydney airport, you should see the Sydney Harbour Bridge, affectionately called 'The Coat Hanger,' and maybe the Sydney Opera House. Throughout the world Sydney is known for these two great structures.

Now bridges are built to provide a connection between two sides of a river or harbour. The Sydney Harbour Bridge does just that - it provides a way to get from one side of the harbour to the other. Recently a tunnel 2.3 km long, and costing $AU 554,000,000 was constructed under the harbour. We are told that the tunnel is safe, and can withstand an earthquake or a ship that might sink to the bottom of the harbour, above or near the tunnel.

Those links remind me of the only link between sinners and God - the Lord Jesus Christ! When we pray to God we do so in the name of our Saviour. The Apostle Paul, writing to Timothy said: 'For there is one God and one Mediator between God and men, the Man Christ Jesus...' (1 Timothy 2:5). Jesus is the perfect Mediator because he is both God and man in the one Person. He understands our difficulties and presents our prayers to his heavenly Father. And all of God's blessings come to Christians through their Lord.

But let us return to the Coat Hanger which is the largest steel arched bridge in the world, but not the longest. Its total length, including the roadway is 1,149 metres, which includes the 503 metres under the arch.

The top of the arch is 134 metres above sea level and the roadway is 75 metres below the archway. This means that almost all ships can sail under the roadway. The bridge has two railway lines, eight lanes for vehicles, a walkway and a separate lane for bicycles.

Painting the bridge uses 270,000 litres of paint and as soon as the painting is completed, the men start all over again. The arch was built from both sides of the harbour and on 19 August, 1930 at 10:00 pm the two sections met and were bolted together. The roadway was then lowered from the arch. This section was completed on 21 January, 1932. In February of that year the bridge was tested. Trains and vehicles were placed in a variety of places and all went well. The weight of everything was far greater than the bridge would normally carry at any one time.

The opening ceremony was spectacular - one never to be forgotten. On 19 March, 1932 a great number of people

- some suggest they numbered between 500,000 and 1,000,000 - were present to witness Mr 'Jack' Lang, the Premier of N.S.W. cut the ribbon. After his speech, with scissors in his hand, he moved forward to cut the ribbon.

Then came the unexpected! A man, dressed in army uniform and riding a horse, spurred forward and with his sabre cut the ribbon. Quickly the police caught him, the ribbon was tied together and this time Mr Lang did the cutting; but it was Captain Francis De Groot who first cut the ribbon. He

was soon released. Those were Depression days, when many people were out of work and governments didn't know what to do to solve the problem of unemployment. De Groot belonged to a group of people who disagreed with Mr Lang's policies, and this was their dramatic way of letting the people of Australia know their feelings.

There was 58,000 tonnes of steel used in building the bridge and 6,000,000 steel rivets of differing sizes. Some 1,400 people were employed, with sixteen men being killed

in accidents while at work. And the bridge moves according to the daily temperature! The archway moves about 18 cm each day and the roadway 42 cm.

Some 'daredevil' pilots have flown their aeroplanes under the bridge and in 1943 twenty four Wirraways set out to do just that. Twenty three were successful, but at the last moment one pilot changed his mind and flew over the bridge instead.

Motorists pay a toll to cross over into the city, and this money is used to keep the bridge in good repair. Cars once had to stop while the toll was paid, but now it is possible to drive across the bridge with a computer keeping a record of each car. Each month an account is forwarded to the car owner.

Now if you want a great adventure and are courageous, you are able, for a price, to walk over the archway, a distance of approximately 1,500 metres. If you do that, you will be able to see Sydney and get some excellent photos to take home with you. But you can count me out as I fear heights!

The Opera House

Not far from the Harbour Bridge you will see the Sydney Opera House, which is claimed to be one of the seven wonders of our age. Arthur Philip, the first Governor of the settlement in 1788, said Sydney Harbour was 'the finest harbour in the world.' He claimed that one thousand ships could move about there in perfect safety.

The Opera House was built on Bennelong Point, named after one of the natives who became very friendly with Governor Philip. It has been used as a fortress, a tram depot, a bus station and now the Opera House. It was Joern Utzon's plan that won the design competition. The building involved work that had not been attempted before, but after much planning the building was completed in 1973 at the cost of $AU 102,000,000. In all, the project took sixteen years of intricate work to complete. This made sure that the acoustics would be as near perfect as possible. The architects made use of the acoustics in the Cathedral Cave which is one of the Jenolan Caves which we will visit later. Each year there are approximately 3,000 events held in the Opera House.

The design was made to look like a sailing ship with a full wind in her sails. The outside shells are covered with more than one million tiles, and the roof is held together using 350 km of steel cable. There are four auditoriums for music, ballet, drama and film. The building which measures 185 metres in length and 120 metres in width, has more than 1,000 rooms. Electric cables measure 645 km, while glass for windows measure approximately 6,225 square metres.

Queen Elizabeth II opened the Opera House, and the first performance in the magnificent building was Prokofiev's 'War and Peace.'

When I hear the wonderful singing coming from today's best musicians I think of the time when all of God's people

will together sing his praise. In Revelation 5:9 and 10 we read of the glory of heaven when praise is sung to Christ:

'You are worthy to take the scroll, and to open its seals;
For you were slain, and have redeemed us to God by your blood, out of every tribe and tongue and people and nation,
and have made us kings and priests to our God;
and we shall reign on the earth.'

In Revelation 15:3 and 4 we read words that are used to praise God. You may not be the best singer in your church, but if you are a Christian the time will come when you will sing perfect praise to God. That will be a wonderful day!

I hope you've enjoyed your adventure at the Sydney Opera House!

A visit to Katoomba

The next place to visit is the city of Katoomba on the edge of the Blue Mountains, so named because in the distance the mountains looked blue in colour. This, we are told, is caused by the eucalyptus atoms that come from Australia's native gum trees. The first European settlement was made in the Sydney area, but very soon there was a need for extra land. Going north and south along the coastal plain was relatively easy, although those who made the journeys had to fight their way through thick bush and across fast flowing rivers. To the west, the settlers thought there would be good land, but the problem was crossing the Great Dividing Range.

At first, explorers made their way along the valleys, only to find their progress stopped by steep timber covered mountains. It wasn't till 1813 that three men - Blaxland, Wentworth and Lawson, made their way to the top of the mountain range by going up the mountain spurs and through thick scrub. They cut notches every now and again in trees, to make their way home easy. Eventually, from the Blue Mountains, they saw a good land spreading to the west as far as the eye could see.

By 1815 thirty convicts and eight soldiers had constructed a 160 km dirt road, wide enough for two carts. During the six months work, the convicts were given good food and treated almost as equals to those in charge. They had their chains removed and any sick men were told to rest until well again. During the six months no convict bothered to escape.

The western plains were opened and proved of great value for sheep and wheat. When gold was discovered in the 1850s many men and women crossed the Great Dividing Range hoping to find a fortune.

If your mum or dad said you all were going to visit the 'Three Sisters' I don't think you'd be impressed. Australia's Three Sisters are not made of flesh and blood, but are unusual rock formations found at Katoomba in the Blue Mountains.

The Three Sisters are three pillars of Triassic sandstone, standing side by side, their height above sea level being 922 metres, 918 metres and 906 metres.

The local kooris (aborigines) have a legend to explain how

the Three Sisters came into existence. One story is about three sisters, Gunnedoo, Wimlah and Meehni who belonged to the Katoomba tribe. They had fallen in love with members of the Nepean tribe, but their tribal law prevented them marrying. When war broke out between the tribes, an old witch doctor of the Katoomba tribe used his 'magic' to turn the sisters into the rock formations we know as the Three Sisters.

The witchdoctor's scheme was to return them to their former beauty when the war ended, but he was killed and no one knew how to undo the spell. And there the Three Sisters are today, three tall pillars of rock for everyone to see.

We know that those formations are the result of wind

and rain wearing the stone away. There was also that great, worldwide flood in the time of Noah, that caused changes in rock formations. What would have taken millions of years to do, happened in a very short time, maybe only months.

After that flood God did something that when seen, would remind people that he would never again destroy the world by flood. He put a large colourful bow in the sky. We call it a Rainbow. This reminds us of God's promise and his faithfulness. How will the world be destroyed next time? (See 2 Peter 3:10-13.) Are you ready for the return of Christ Jesus?

There is a lot to do at Katoomba. When you go to the fenced viewing platform to see the Three Sisters you are standing at 'Echo Point.' While there you can call out in your loudest voice, and you will clearly hear the echo of what you

said. The cliffs and valleys are covered in bush, where people spend time trekking along the many walks through the scrub, while other very brave people climb from the valley to the mountain top. In the wet season the swiftly flowing creeks and rivers make canoeing a favourite sport.

Some people walk down the Giant Staircase to the place where the scenic railway has its station. Then it's up to the top of the escarpment on what may be the steepest railway to be found anywhere. You will travel at an angle of 52° passing through a rain forest and a tunnel. If you want a very good sight of the valley area, and you have no fear of heights, you can take a journey from one side of the mountain to the other, on a skyway.

The Jenolan Caves

Before leaving the Blue Mountains you should visit the Jenolan Caves at Katoomba. For a fee you will be allowed to walk through a section of the caves, without a guide. These caves have colourful electric lighting and have been given a variety of names including the Grand Arch and The Devil's Coach House. The caves without lighting are very dark and there you will need a guide with a light. You will see sharp limestone projections hanging from the roof and pillars growing upwards from the floor. These formations have names - Stalagmites and Stalactites.

It is believed that the first European to discover the caves was a bushranger named James McKeown. He had no respect for God's law which clearly says: 'You shall not steal' (Exodus 20:15). Frequently he would hold up travellers, and then escape to the caves with his stolen loot. When he robbed James Whalan, the man tracked him to his hideaway. Whalan returned home, armed himself, and accompanied by his brother and two troopers (horseback police) returned to captured the bandit in what became known as McKeown's Hole.

The Whalan brothers then, for a fee, started giving guided tours of the caves. In 1866 the region was proclaimed a reserve with a 'Keeper' appointed to take care of the area.

During the night, native animals can be seen in the caves - the ring-tailed possum, sugar gliders, the boo book owl, kangaroos, wallabies, the spiny ant eater, the wombat and many more of God's creatures.

All too soon your adventure to the Blue Mountains is over and it's back to Sydney for a quick visit to Taronga Park Zoo where you will see two very peculiar mammals.

The Echidna

At Taronga Park Zoo you will see animals from all parts of the world. Among them are two very unusual Australian creatures that lay eggs! No! They are not some strange type of bird but unusual mammals.

First, I'll tell you something about the Echidna, which is usually called 'The Spiny Ant Eater.' It has a curved backbone and a back which is covered with strong, sharp spines. Adults have been known to grow to 50 cm in size, and live for over 35 years.

God designed echidnas so that they can easily protect themselves. Not many animals want to attack echidnas as they usually end up with blood oozing from injuries inflicted by their spines. The Australian dog, the dingo, tries to turn the echidna over and bite into his belly which has no spines, but the echidna quickly digs himself into the ground with his strong feet. If that doesn't work, he rolls himself into a ball of sharp spikes. He also has a razor-sharp spur on his hind legs, which can severely wound any animal foolish enough to attack!

Christians also have an armour to protect them against Satan's demons. The Apostle Paul tells his people to: '...take up the whole armour of God, that you may be able to withstand in the evil day, and having done all, to stand. Stand therefore, having girded your waist with the belt of truth, having put on the breastplate of righteousness, and having put on your feet the shoes of readiness to announce the gospel of peace; above all, taking the shield of faith with which you will be able to quench all the fiery darts of the wicked one. And take the helmet of salvation, and the sword of the Spirit, which is the word of God; praying always ...' (Ephesians 6:13-18).

Christ defeated Satan, and all who love God and have placed their faith in the Lord Jesus, will one day be taken to heaven. Christ has destroyed the fear of death because he has paid what his people owed because of their sins, and has given them his righteousness. God cares for his people even when times are difficult. Remember the words in Romans 8:28: 'And we know that all things work together for good to those who love God, to those who are the called according to His purpose.'

Now Spiny Ant Eaters have that name because they live on a diet of ants and termites. With their strong feet and a long strong snout they are able to break into the nests of ants and termites. As the ants come to the surface to rebuild their nests, the echidna's long, sticky tongue flashes out and soon the ants are in his toothless mouth. The adult echidna has a tongue that extends more than twenty centimetres beyond the end of his snout. Now that's a long tongue which is used to catch food !

We should use our tongue to praise God. Never should it be used for swearing, telling rude stories, or criticising other people.

The echidna is found all over Australia. In the cold months it hibernates and in very hot weather it gets out of the sun by resting under logs, or digging burrows in which to stay.

During July and August the female usually lays just one egg, which is quickly put into her small pouch. About ten days later, the egg hatches, and a tiny echidna, which has milk teeth, hangs onto milk hairs and drinks the milk that oozes through the pores in the mother's pouch.

Fortunately baby echidna has no sharp spines on its body, and remains in its mother's pouch until it starts to grow spines and gets too big and heavy. Then the mother digs a small burrow for her baby and spends her time searching for ants. Every four or five days she returns to her young one, so it can drink mum's milk.

The last echidna I saw was slowly crossing a road. All the cars had stopped to make sure he reached the other side in safety.

The Platypus

The platypus is the second of the Australian mammals to lay an egg. They are found on the east coast of the continent, in lakes and creeks where they can easily find their food - tadpoles, small fish, worms, insects and yabbies. To get their daily meal they take a breath and with eyes closed dive to the bottom of the water, and there poke about until they have a mouth full of delicious food. Their 'bill' (nose and mouth) is very sensitive and they easily find food. In captivity in the zoos, the platypus averages about sixty dives an hour.

The adult grows to about 50 cm from the tip of his tail to the end of his bill. They have webbed feet making swimming easy. The fur on their back is a dark brown, while underneath it is a silky grey colour, both colours giving them some protection from predators.

They use their front, webbed feet for swimming and their hind, webbed feet for steering. On both hind feet they have a poisonous spur which causes much pain and swelling to any creature, including humans, they consider to be a danger.

The mother lays one to three eggs in a nest at the end of

a long burrow found at the edge of creeks or lakes, many being more than ten metres in length with an opening below water level. Each egg is almost 2 cm in length and after nine or ten days, hatch into small (2.5 cm), blind, hairless babies who drink the milk that oozes from their mothers' milk pores. The mothers gradually introduce them to adult food, and after three or four months they are taught to search for their own daily food.

In the early days of European settlement, both the platypus and echidna were trapped for food and the platypus for his skin and fur. Today they are protected animals.

It is wonderful how God has given these lovely creatures all they need to live. We should always thank God when we sit down to our daily meals. In the Lord's Prayer we say: 'Give us this day our daily bread' (Matthew 6:11). I'm sure very few of us realise what a blessing it is to have our food, all of which comes from a God of grace. Does your family say grace before or after your meals? I hope so, but if not, now is the time to start. And always mean what you pray.

Captain Cook

All too soon it's time to continue your journey north. From Sydney airport you'll travel by QANTAS to Cairns. First it is a good idea to see the reef areas from a large catamaran giving you an idea of the 'big picture.' There are many holiday destinations found on the G.B.R., where you can make trips in glass bottomed boats through which you have a good sight of the coral, seaweed and fish. Many holiday islands have constructed under water aquariums, where you are able to see the creatures face to face. The walls are made from strong glass, well able to withstand the water pressure.

I want to tell you a true story that happened well over two hundred years ago. The great explorer, Captain James Cook, had found his way to the northern region of Australia, 'the Great South Land.' He had no real idea of the water depths and what lay under his boat which was named the 'Endeavour.'

The sailors were carefully making their way through the islands and reefs along the eastern coast, when at 11:00 pm on 11th June, 1770, the Endeavour came to a sudden stop.

The boat was not only holed, but was stuck fast on the reef with waves pounding its side. To lighten the ship, the crew threw about fifty tons of cargo overboard, including the boat's cannons. The spot was marked, so Cook could, if possible, return at a later date and retrieve the guns.

At high tide more goods were thrown overboard, while men worked the pumps. Fortunately the following day the

coral broke away and the ship was free. The hole in the Endeavour was plugged with the lump of coral, which helped prevent the ship sinking. Cook then decided to 'fother' the ship. (This was a new word to me also!) He had several sailors swim under the ship, pulling a sail which contained a lump of wool and oakum. When this mixture reached the hole it acted as a plug making it possible to beach the Endeavour, and make repairs. This place is now called Cooktown. Captain Cook named the river where the repairs were carried out, 'Endeavour River.'

Cook was probably the best British sailor at that time, and was able to do what was necessary to save all on board his ship.

In many respects your minister is like a Captain Cook. He must be always ready to point out the way of salvation to his congregation, and others, who come to him for spiritual help. Do you know the only way to become God's friend? Remember, you are a sinner and our holy God detests sin and the unrepentant sinner. We read in the Scriptures: 'Believe on the Lord Jesus Christ, and you will be saved, you and your household' (Acts 16:31). To become God's friend we must have a saving faith in Christ and show that we do by obeying God's commands in the Bible. We will fail to obey many times, but remember that: 'If we confess our sins, He is faithful and just to forgive us our sins and to cleanse us from all unrighteousness' (1 John 1:9).

Lost at sea

Before taking the boat to your holiday resort, many people have a catamaran trip to see places of interest. When the boat reaches the shallow water where schools of coloured fish swim about the reef, passengers often don their diving gear and get into the water for a closer look. On one occasion a very excited boat load of tourists arrived at a spot where the brightly coloured coral and fish could be clearly seen.

Everyone was having a pleasant time, but all too soon the Captain, using the loudspeaker, called those in the water to return to the boat for the return trip back to Cairns. When the boat arrived at the Cairns' wharf, the Captain was horrified to find that two people were missing - they had been left behind!

As soon as the call for help was sounded several helicopters left immediately for the area where the passengers had been scuba diving. The Water Police also left for the area. The result was tragic. The two tourists, a man and his wife, were never found. Now all tourists on similar jaunts have their names carefully checked before the boat departs for home.

In your Bible, in Matthew 25:1-13 there is a parable about some young women who were left behind - but this was not because someone forgot about them. The story tells us about ten young women. Five of these girls were wise and five were foolish. Five girls were ready for the bridegroom and five were not. The five who were ready went to the wedding but the five who were not ready were left behind and in the end they didn't get to join in the celebrations. In this story Christ was teaching that he would one day return to earth, to take his people to be with him for ever.

The five girls who were ready represent God's people. God's people love the Lord and are anxiously awaiting his return in power and glory. They find pleasure in worshipping their Saviour. Daily they read the Scriptures and gave time to prayer. By God's grace they turn their backs on their

old sinful ways, and having been born again, live a life of righteousness.

What joy it will be to see our Saviour face to face, and with the other saints, take our places in the new heavens and earth he has prepared for his people.

The parable also speaks of those who were left behind. Five girls were not ready. Make sure you are prepared and ready for the return of Christ.

Now, back to our pleasant journey to the coral reef. Frequently the ship's captain makes his way to a nearby island where there is a barbecue prepared for everyone. Usually it is a barbecue of the best meat and fish available, with all the salad vegetables you could possibly eat. While you are eating, the guide talks about the reef and what you will be doing during your stay in the guest house.

It certainly is an exciting adventure.

Great Barrier Reef Fish

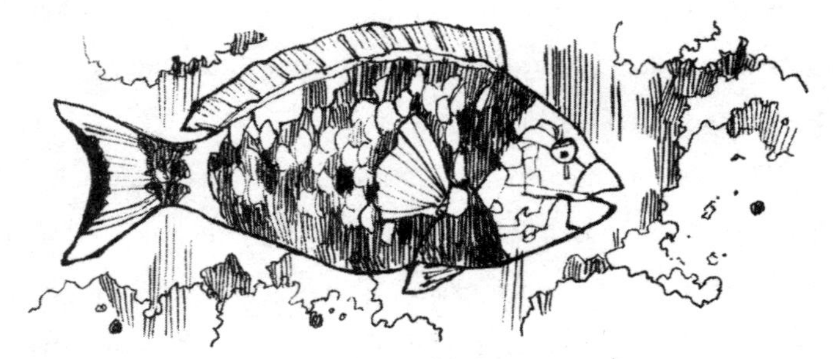

It is not possible to tell you about the approximately 2,800 species of the fish that swim in the waters about the coral reef, adding to the beauty of the multicoloured underwater garden. God created everything and I sometimes wonder why our God, who is spirit, created creatures made of flesh and blood. He created colour, smell, sight, taste and hearing in his creation. All of this displays our Lord's majesty, power, wisdom, and glory.

Why then did God create fish with so many colours? As well as providing beauty, their colour blends in with the colours of the coral, giving them protection from predators.

I will tell you about some unusual fish; some that I didn't know existed until I started reading about the G.B.R.

The parrot fish, usually found in schools, with as many as two hundred members, feed on algae. They are brightly coloured, feeding during the day and resting at night. This fish has a mouth like a beak which it uses to break into the coral for food.

Other fish, such as the brightly coloured butterfly fish,

have a dark spot on the tail end of their body. To predators, this looks like the eye of the fish and when attacked, the fish is able to make a quick escape. Many of this species are able to change their colour when danger is sensed.

Another unusual fish is the mudskipper. In 1770 Captain Cook and his crew saw the unusual mudskippers jumping about in the mud like frogs. They are able to make their way out of the water, and onto the mud flats looking for food - insects and crustations. They use their fin legs to move about, and with a good flick of their tail, they can leap about a metre. As long as their gills are moist, they can survive out of water for a long time.

There are other fish that can change their sex - a male today and for some reason a female sometime later.

One fish that really amazed me was the vividly coloured Teuthidae, which has several nicknames - the 'surgeon fish' or the 'doctor fish.' It is hard to imagine that these fish are 'doctors.' Fish with medical problems approach the place where the surgeon fish is to be found and wait their turn to be treated. The sick fish act strangely - rolling onto their sides or floating in an unusual position. The brightly coloured

doctor fish, comes out and commences his surgical work, which includes removing parasites and treating any infected sores. With big fish they are known to swim into its mouth to treat infections. Do you believe all this? I found it hard to believe, but it is true!

Doctor fish have been known to treat as many as three hundred fish in a day! So far twenty one species of fish, one crab, one worm and six types of shrimps have been discovered carrying out their medical work. These creatures play an

important role in the daily sea life - and the patients are not given an account! Apparently there are hypochondriac fish who wait to be treated, but the doctor fish recognises them and leaves them alone.

Isn't the interaction between fish amazing?

The doctor fish reminded me of my Saviour who lived and died, to make it possible for his people to go to heaven. I was once covered with the most deadly disease - unforgiven sins. Had I died I would have spent eternity in hell. However, the best and only doctor for sin is our Saviour, the Lord Jesus Christ.

In Jeremiah we find the prophet directing people to the 'Balm in Gilead' (8:22). Jeremiah uses this as a picture to describe God who is the only one who can remove the sickness of sin. Christ invited his people: 'Come to Me, all you who labour and are heavy laden, and I will give you rest. Take My yoke upon you and learn from Me, for I am gentle and lowly in heart, and you will find rest for your souls. For My yoke is easy and My burden is light." (Matthew 11:28-30).

Here is the answer to sin - 'Believe on the Lord Jesus Christ and you shall be saved!' (Acts 16:31).

Adventurers, go to your Bible and as you read, pray that God will give you a saving knowledge of the Redeemer.

Great Barrier Reef Birds

Many birds live on islands along the G.B.R., but most of these, like the seagull, are found in many parts of the world. Those living on the reef islands normally have a white body, with grey feathered wings. They are scavengers that quickly devour scraps of food lying about. They come in droves to fight over a handful of prawns and watch closely while you are cleaning fish, hoping to be the one to catch the intestines, when they are thrown away. While you are on holidays the seagulls will soon become your friends.

Do you have many friends? I trust that you are one of Christ's friends; but how can a sinful person become God's friend? Jesus commanded sinners to repent of their sins and trust him alone for their salvation. He said: 'Greater love has no one than this, than to lay down one's life for his friends.' This was exactly what he was about to do. Christ then went on to say: 'You are My friends if you do whatever I command you' (John 15: 13, 14). Read your Bible and you will find the law of God. By the grace of God obey his law. The reason Christians want to obey God's law is to show how thankful they are for what Christ has done for them - ie. saved them from the penalty of their sin. When you fail to be obedient, pray that he will forgive you for Jesus' sake.

Now back to the birds ... Sometimes as you look out to sea, you will notice a bird diving into the water and coming out with a fish in its claws. This is the osprey. I read that sometimes the osprey comes to grief by plunging to catch a big fish. Its claws clutch the fish, but the bird is unable to fly because of the weight of its catch. There are times when both die because the osprey's claws cannot release the fish.

The tern is a common bird with a variety of colours. Some look like a yellow beaked seagull with a black hat. In the northern regions of the G.B.R. you will find what is called a sooty tern. They have the nickname 'Wideawakes' because their call, made during the night sounds like 'wideawake.'

Another has the nickname of 'Dog Tern.' This is because their cry is like the yapping of a dog. Near Green Island there is a colony of thousands of these birds during nesting time. When the nesting time is over they fly away, only to return to the same spot when it is again nesting time. They catch their food by diving into the ocean and catching fish.

You will also see the Reef Heron which is either white or dark in colour. They build their nests in trees near the water's edge, and catch their food in shallow water. They have quite long legs and beak. Many years ago the heron was trapped during the mating season for its white neck feathers. Those feathers were called 'ospreys' and used to decorate women's hats. These birds are now protected.

Another bird that divebombs the ocean water to catch fish is the gannet. Within this species are birds of a variety of colours. A close relative is the pelican who has a huge bill. An adult pelican, from wing tip to wing tip may be three metres. When a flock is flying they usually do so in a V formation. They will hunt fish together, driving them into shallow water and then scooping them up into their huge bill.

The final bird is one I didn't know existed - the frigate bird. Sometimes they fly very quickly and at other times simply ride the air currents, hovering in one spot. They would be better known as 'pirate fish,' because they wait until a bird carrying food for their young returns from a day's fishing. The frigate bird then attacks the one with the fish, and keeps attacking until the poor bird drops its meal or disgorges the food it had for its chick.

The frigate (pirate) bird then eats his meal without having done any work.

The Apostle Paul wrote to some lazy Christians at Thessalonica: 'If anyone will not work, neither shall he eat' (2 Thessalonians 3: 10).

Those Christians had given up working, as they believed Christ was about to return. Those foolish Christians began asking their Christian brothers and sisters for food. Paul's answer was plain. If you can work, and there is a vacancy, you take on the job; if not, don't expect others to give you food. Our obligation to give help is when there is genuine need.

Most holiday resorts have someone whose work is to keep young people occupied. You will have plenty of time to swim in the protected clear, blue waters about the island. Most places have tennis courts where you will be able to have a game with other young tourists. If you would like, you could try some snorkelling and really get close to the fish and coral. With some training you might also try scuba diving.

Body surfing is good fun and I'm sure you'd find surfboards to use in the waves that come crashing on the shore. Maybe you'll try riding a sailboard. The winds are usually quite strong, especially in the afternoon and you will get along at a quick speed, but make sure you know how to get back to your starting point - you don't want to end up in New Zealand! A new surfing activity is riding a surfboard while hanging on to a kite. In strong winds the surfer and his surfboard move along at great speed. Frequent very strong gusts of wind lift both rider and surfboard out of the water for a short distance.

With all the different activities I'm sure every adventurer will sleep soundly!

Unpleasant fish

There are some unpleasant creatures living in the water about the G.B.R. The first of these is the shark. Many scuba divers come face to face with the grey reef shark. While it might scare the diver, a fully grown one is about two metres in length and not interested in humans for food. However, like all sharks, it will protect itself if provoked. There is the blacktip reef shark, also largely harmless, although it has been known to bite the foot or leg of someone wading through the coral.

There are several sharks that must be avoided - the tiger and hammerhead. While they tend to spend their time in deep water, they can and do sometimes attack divers. As I was writing these words I heard a newsflash telling of a shark attack in the northern section of the G.B.R. A diver was attacked by a big tiger shark which tore off one leg. He bled to death before help arrived.

There are many sea creatures that look attractive, yet cause great pain, and even death to those who get in their way. Satan and his followers do the same. They make sin appear exciting and delightful, but sin's wages are death. Just because someone seems to be doing and saying what appears reasonable, we must be on guard, for we are warned about Satan: 'For such are false apostles, deceitful workers, transforming themselves into apostles of Christ. And no wonder! For Satan himself transforms himself into an angel of light. Therefore it is no great thing if his ministers also transform themselves into ministers of righteousness, whose end will be according to their works. (2 Cor 11:13-15). We are to imitate those Bereans of old who received the word with all readiness, and searched the Scriptures daily to find out whether they were told the truth (Acts 17:11). Do you ever check what you are taught at Sunday School and church to see if it is truth.

Found in the warm coastal waters, is the Box Jellyfish. They are to be avoided at all times, as their sting usually results in death. Its name comes from the fact that it has the shape of a cube whose sides can grow to over 30 cm in length. From each corner of the open side it has as many as fifteen tentacles,

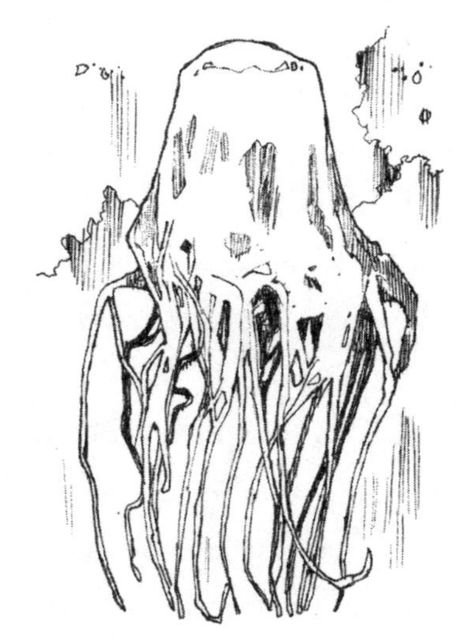

which can grow to 9 metres in length. In the summer months they are found in greater numbers at the seashore. They have a life span of over two hundred days, and can move in the water in whatever direction they choose. Marine biologists have determined they can travel at 5 km/hour. They have eyes that are used to find food, usually small shrimps and fish which are stung with some of the multitude of stings along their tentacles.

Their sting is so severe that a human can die within several minutes. Some popular beaches have nets around the swimming areas to prevent the box jellyfish from harming swimmers. Many beaches have vinegar in a first aid kit that prevents stinging cells from releasing more poison. Then it's an urgent trip to the hospital.

The box jellyfish is considered the most venomous animal found in the sea. In Australia over seventy people have been killed by this creature. However, they do have enemies, one being the green turtle that swallows them down like we eat chocolate. My wife,Val, and I had a holiday at Cairns, and we did all our swimming in the motel pool. We were warned about the box jellyfish in the ocean and crocodiles in the river. We decided that if we were to die because of one of those creatures they would have to travel a few miles over land to find us!

The Stone Fish also lives here. They have this name because they live on the seabed and look like a stone. They grow to about 30 cm and are ugly to look at. Most of the time they are hard to see and anyone walking about the coral reef at low tide must be very careful. Some are just a couple of centimetres below the water level, while others are completely out of the water. They have thirteen poisonous spines along their back and if trodden on cause extreme pain.

The Giant Toado has large, strong teeth which have been known to bite through hooks on a fisherman's line. In 1980 a couple of children, walking in shallow water, were attacked by this fish, that bit several toes from one child's foot. For some time the local children refused to go into the water at Shute Harbour, until the fish was caught (See Robert Endean's 'Australia's Great Barrier Reef.')

There is also the Zebra-fish (lion fish) which is covered in a variety of coloured fins. They live in their selected area of the seabed, and spend time patrolling the area. When they see an intruder they attack. Like the pain from the Stone Fish it is extreme and can last for days. The poison can also effect breathing and cause paralysis. If you are stung you should wash the area with very hot water, and go to a doctor immediately.

Amongst the rocks and coral you might find an octopus. It is pleasant to look at, as it is normally brown and yellow. However, if it fears danger, it changes its colour to blue markings - hence its name 'The Blue Ringed Octopus.' Like every octopus it has eight legs, but this one has a beak strong enough to bite through a wet-suit. Its poison affects the nerves and very quickly the person's breathing is affected. The poison is so strong that it can kill a person in several minutes. The lesson about this octopus is - Don't touch it at all - just look!

The sting from the above creatures, and others, can cause great distress, even death. Sin is like that! When we violate

God's law it causes distress and we must seek forgiveness. To approach death without a saving faith in the Lord Jesus would be terrible - and frightening! The Apostle Paul wrote that 'the sting of death is sin,' but he went on to write: 'But thanks be to God, who gives us the victory through our Lord Jesus Christ' (1 Corinthians 15:56, 57).

God gives sinners the victory through the Saviour. We can face whatever the future might hold because we are united to him by faith - all of our sins have been forgiven.

Another creature that can cause pain is the Manta Ray, sometimes called the Devil Ray. These fish can grow to a width of seven metres and weigh 1,500 kg. They give birth to live babies which are about 1.5 metres in width and weigh

11 kg. They swim about in schools and sometimes come to the surface of the water and jump out. Some rays, if trodden on can inflict serious, painful wounds.

Along the reef you will find clams of various sizes. You may have read about the giant clams (bivalves) that have snapped shut upon the leg of a pearl diver, holding him tight until his oxygen runs out and he dies.

There are other bivalves that produce pearls. Pearl searching is hard work, but now we find that cultured pearls are produced in pearl farms when a small object is placed in a 'golden-lip' bivalve.

This reminds me of Christ's parable of the pearl of great price: 'Again, the kingdom of heaven is like a merchant seeking beautiful pearls, who, when he had found one pearl of great price, went and sold all that he had and bought it' (Matthew 13: 45, 46). Here the Lord is explaining that salvation is worth everything we have. We must be ready and willing if necessary to give away all of our possessions, to have Christ as our Redeemer. Read the story of the rich young man whose earthly treasures were of greater value to him than treasure in heaven. (Matthew 19:16-26).

Christ is so precious that we should be willing to sacrifice everything for him. Nothing should stand in the way.

Reef attack

There are many seastars living about the G.B.R. They belong to the echinoderm family - starfish, sea urchins and sea cucumbers. To open bivalves, such as oysters, you need a knife as they have very strong muscles. However, the members of the echinoderm family have feet like small tubes, which are used to open the bivalves. They move towards their victim, and wrap themself about the shell. Then they start to pull the shell apart. Soon the muscles of the bivalve begin to tire and its flesh can be seen. The seastar can't chew and swallow its food, so they push their stomach out over the flesh and then digest their meal. When all the food is gone, they pull their stomach back into the safety of their body and start looking for their next meal.

There is a rather large starfish known as the 'Crown-of-thorns starfish.' This creature has between twelve and eighteen tentacles that grow to about 20cm in length. Its food is live coral, and you can imagine the damage that is being done to the reef, as this creature eats polyps. It holds on to the coral, while its stomach comes out and slowly digests the polyps before moving on to the next mouthful.

The crown-of-thorns breed at a tremendous rate. In summer, the female lays as many as several million eggs which are fertilized by the male. Those that are fertilized float along on the ocean surface, until they sink down and begin eating the polyps.

The crown-of-thorns reminds me of the Lord Jesus wearing that terrible crown of thorns that was made by the Roman soldiers, who laughed at the 'KING OF KINGS AND LORD OF LORDS' (Revelation 19:16). My Saviour suffered hell for me and all of his people. Has he done so for you?

Marine biologists are spending a lot of time trying to

discover a method of killing the crown-of-thorns without causing harm to other parts of the reef. It is believed that humans are largely to blame for their great increase in numbers. The triton mollusc enjoys eating the crown-of-thorns, but their numbers have decreased over the years. Why?

The triton shells were once very popular and it is estimated that between 1947 and 1960 ten thousand were taken. It is now illegal for anyone to remove that shell.

Of course when people visit the reef for a holiday, they walk over the coral at low tide and destroy parts of reef. Tourists are warned that they cannot remove coral, as there are shops where they can buy dead coral pieces that have been painted to give the appearance of living coral.

Most holiday resorts have underwater caverns where tourists can see the inhabitants of the reef through glass. You are also able to take a trip in a glass bottomed boat which gives everyone a good view of the coral and fish living in the area. Tourists are able to scuba dive, where they swim with the fish and see first hand what the reef is really like.

Shipping through the G.B.R. can cause great damage. In 1998 almost six thousand boats over fifty metres in length passed through the area. There is always the possibility of an oil spill. All ships are required to give information to the authorities of the route they plan to take, and then a careful watch is taken to prevent any damage to coral. In some areas, ships must have a licensed pilot on board to ensure the region is not damaged. The Australian Government has had beacons erected, again to ensure the safe passage of ships through the reef.

It is believed that oil is to be found in the reef region and some companies are trying to obtain permission to commence drilling. Other problems to the reef include severe coastal flooding which causes chemicals used in farming and other industries being washed out to sea. Polyps can't live in fresh water and are killed by the fresh water in times of flood.

Commercial fishing takes place about the reef and it is estimated that 1,500 tonnes of fish are taken annually. Added to this is the large quantity of fish taken by amateur fishermen. This has been blamed for the smaller numbers of fish being found in some areas. However, the G.B.R. is under the care of the Great Barrier Reef Marine Authority, which hands out very big fines to companies, or individuals who disobey the laws made to protect the whole area.

Our God has laws that must be obeyed by every person born on this earth - the ten commandments. And we break those laws again and again. The Apostle Paul wrote of the punishment for everyone who disobeyed God: 'For the wages of sin is death' (Romans 6:23). He went on to say that God's gift to repentant sinners, who turn to Jesus Christ is eternal life.

May you be one of those people spoken about in John 3:16, the 'whoever' people: 'For God so loved the world that He gave His only begotten Son, that whoever believes in Him should not perish but have everlasting life.'

Time to go home

A lovely way to view the Whitsunday area of the G.B.R. is to hire a small yacht and sail around the beautiful islands. It was Captain James Cook who gave the name of 'Whitsunday' to the region because he believed he sailed into the area on Whitsunday. Whitsunday is the name given by some churches to the seventh Sunday after Easter - the day of Pentecost when the Holy Spirit came in power to the church.

The Holy Spirit's power can be seen in your own life too when you repent and believe in Jesus Christ. You can't do this on your own - you can only do this with the help of the Holy Spirit. How can you get the Holy Spirit's help - by praying to God and asking him to give you his help (Romans 2:4; Luke 11:13).

Captain Cook made an error as his log was one day out in the date. He had failed to note the Endeavour's crossing of the International Date Line. Maybe you could find out all you can about the International Date Line.

Other tourists book a passage on a larger vessel. One of these yachts has the name 'Gretel.' Gretel was the Australian yacht that sailed in the America's Cup.

This type of a holiday can be great fun. You have your own family cabin and the best of food, all of which is cooked on board by the ship's cook. There is a planned tour route making it possible for visits to be made to various islands where souvenirs can be purchased. Visits are made to uninhabited islands where everyone can take a leisurely walk about. Time is usually set aside for some fishing, snorkelling and scuba diving. You may be given the opportunity to climb the mast and help with the duties of a sailor.

Sometimes a strong net is lowered from the bow of the yacht to the tip of the prow and then lowered into the water. Anyone who wants some excitement jumps overboard and into the water as it gushes through the net.

Holidaying on a yacht is usually a very exciting and pleasant adventure; but a friend who was with his family, booked on a four day trip, declared he would never have such a holiday

again. He said that almost all the time on board he wished that he was dead. Why?

He was seasick all the time! The rest of the family felt great, but poor Dad just wanted to get his two feet back on the land. I hope you've had a better experience on your adventures along the East Coat of Australia and especially the Great Barrier Reef.

May God bless all who read this book.

Great Barrier Reef Quiz

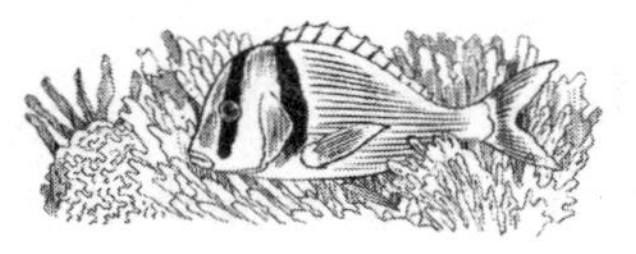

1. What are a polyps buds filled with?

2. What plant does God tell us to 'consider' and why?

3. Who started the flying doctor service?

4. How did Jesus enter the city of Jerusalem?

5. Trick question! What fairies live near London Bridge?

6. Jesus Christ is a rock of refuge and a fortress of -------?

7. What is the nick name for Sydney Harbour Bridge?

8. Who is the only link between sinners and God?

9. Who opened the Sydney Opera House?

10. Who should we sing praise to?

11. What was discovered across the Great Dividing Range in the 1850's?

12. What does the rainbow remind us of?

13. What animal in this chapter had a ringtail?

14. What commandment did the bushranger, James McKeown, regularly break?

15. Name one mammal that lays eggs.

16. Name two pieces of the Christian's armour.

17. Name one other mammal who lays eggs.

18. What do we ask God for in Matthew 6:11?

19. What was the name of Captain Cook's ship?

20. What do we need to become God's friend?

21. What is a reef made out of?

22. What event does Jesus tell us to be ready for?

23. Approximately how may species of fish swim in the Great Barrier Reef?

24. What is the deadliest disease that Jesus saves us from?

25. What 'yapping' bird lives near Green Island?

26. Why do Christians what to obey God's law?

27. What store cupboard ingredient can be used to treat a jellyfish sting?

28. What are the wages of sin?

29. Name a large starfish that eats live coral.

30. What is God's gift to repentant sinners who turn to Christ?

31. How did Captain Cook make a mistake in naming the area of Whitsunday?

32. Can you repent and believe in Jesus Christ on your own without any help?

Answers

1. Eggs.

2. The Lily – it doesn't toil or spin but it looks even better than the splendid King Solomon. So we shouldn't worry about our clothes.

3, Rev. John Flynn.

4. On a donkey.

5. Fairy penguins live near the rock formation on London Bridge.

6. Defense.

7. The Coat Hanger.

8. The Lord Jesus.

9. Queen Elizabeth II.

10. Jesus Christ/God.

11. Gold.

12. God's promise and faithfulness.

13. Possum.

14. The Eighth – You shall not steal.

15. The Spiry Ant Eater or Echidna.

16. Belt of Truth; Breastplate of Righteousness; Shoes of Readiness; Shield of Faith; Helmet of Salvation; Sword of the Spirit.

17. Duck Billed Platypus.

18. Our daily bread.
19. The Endeavour.
20. A saving faith in Christ.
21. Billions of small sea creatures called polyps.
22. His return.
23. 2,800.
24. Sin.
25. Dog Tern
26. To show God they are thankful for what Christ has done.
27. Vinegar.
28. Death.
29. The Crown-of-thorns.
30. Eternal life.
31. He thought he entered that area on Whit Sunday, the seventh Sunday after Easter, but he was wrong - he didn't take into account the International Date Line.
32. No, you need the help of the Holy Spirit.

0
500 mls
0
800 kmls
Hall's
Creek
Indian
Ocean
Western Australia
Perth
N

Great Barrier Reef
Pacific Ocean
Great Divide Range
Great Barrier Reef
Alice Springs
Queensland
Brisbane
Bald Rock
Lake Eyre
New South Wales
Sydney
Canberra
A.C.I.
(Australian Capital Territory)
Victoria
Melbourne
Bass Strait
Tasmania
Hobart

If you enjoyed this book make sure you read:

OUTBACK ADVENTURES
by Jim Cromarty

The Australiain outback is the place to be if you want to find out about Kangaroos, wallabies, emus and the amazing rock formations and scenery that this hot, wild landscape offers you. If you enjoyed reading about the God who made the mudskipper and the Surgeon fish there are many more Aussie Animals to discover in the Outback!

Outback Adventures by Jim Cromarty
ISBN 1-85792-974-8

The Adventures Series
An ideal series to collect.

Have you ever wanted to visit the rainforest? Have you ever longed to sail down the Amazon river? Would you just love to go on Safari in Africa? Well, these books can help you imagine that you are actually there.

Pioneer missionaries retell their amazing adventures and encounters with animals and nature. In the Amazon you will discover tree frogs, piranha fish and electric eels. In the Rainforest you will be amazed at the armadillo and the toucan. In the blistering heat of the African Savannah you will come across lions and elephants and hyenas. And you will discover how God is at work in these amazing environments.

Rainforest Adventures by Horace Banner
ISBN 1-85792-4401
Amazon Adventures by Horace Banner
ISBN 1-85792-6277
African Adventures by Dick Anderson
ISBN 1-85792-8075
Rocky Mountain Adventures by Betty Swinford
ISBN 1-85792-962-4
Outback Adventures by Jim Cromarty
ISBN 1-85792-974-8

Sample Chapter from the latest in this series:

Himalayan Adventures

by Penny Reeve

ISBN 1-84550-080-6

Nepal is quite a small country, it is shaped like a sausage with the northern border hidden in the Himalayas and the southern border running along vast flat plains. In between the plains and the mountains are the valleys and hills and it is in this area of Nepal, in the lower foothills of the Himalayas, 1000 metres above sea level, that the Chepang people live.

The Chepang people are one of Nepal's many ethnic groups. They have their own language and many unique customs. Unlike other people groups who like to build their villages in clusters and groups, the Chepang people scatter the homes in their villages along the ridges of hills. If they look up they can see the mountains that make Nepal famous. If they look down they can see the Terai and India. All around them are deep gorges and steep rivers and the jungle in which the tree the Chepang call Yershi grows.

The Yershi is a very big tree with large leaves. The branches spread out like a canopy leaving the underneath bare, cool and shaded. In winter the tree flowers and at the end of the branches clusters of small creamy yellow flowers appear which are full of sweet nectar. When the flowers fall off the tree they have a hollow centre through which you can thread a stick or a string. After the flowers come the nuts which can be ground and steamed and eaten which is probably why another name for the tree is Indian Butternut. But, if you take

one Yershi tree, and a pitch black night, you could go hunting with the Chepang.

The Chepang are expert bat hunters. In the middle of a winter night they get up and take their nets. Then, following the jungle paths they have memorized, they find a Yershi tree laden with flowers. If I was to go with them I am sure I would trip and fall down some steep hillside, but they know their jungle so well they can travel this way even in the dark. Once they reach the tree they set up their nets strung open wide between a bamboo pole and the tree. One end of the net is secured firmly to the ground and tree, the other is attached to the pole held by a hunter further away. Once the invisible wall of netting is installed under the tree's canopy the hunters then wait. Perfectly still and perfectly quiet they sit, hoping that when the bats do arrive their squealing will not attract leopards.

Some bats in the Himalayan region eat fruit, others eat insects and bugs and still others eat nectar. It is the nectar eating bats which come to feed from the flowers in the Yershi tree. They suck out the sweet nectar as their main source of food, not realizing that tonight they will be caught and become food themselves. As the bats fly under the tree they fly straight into the Chepang nets. The person holding the pole then swings it around, closing the net and trapping the bat between the folds of net. Then the bat is pulled down, the net opened again, and another bat caught. Sometimes, on a good night, the Chepang hunters can catch up to 20 bats under one tree. And that means a great meal.

While I was hearing about the way the Chepang people hunt bats under the Yershi tree, I couldn't help thinking about the Creator of our world. He didn't just make things here and there and hope that, by chance, they would all work together nicely. No, the Yershi tree makes beautiful nectar, the nectar attracts the bats who in turn fertilize the tree while they eat. The tree is nice and tall with an easy canopy underneath, perfect for hoisting up a net. And the Chepang catch some of the bats to supplement their diet with added protein. Isn't it great that when we trust God, we are trusting a God who has a plan and a purpose for everything? He knows what we need to grow and live. He knows what makes Yershi trees flower and why bats like the sweet nectar - because that is how He created the world. Nothing was an accident. Everything in creation has His signature on it. Even Yershi trees and nectar-eating bats and people like you and me.

In the beginning God created the heavens and the earth. God saw all that he had made, and it was very good. Genesis 1:1 and 31

Torchbearers

People who had courage and faith

Margaret, Agnes and Thomas have to run from the King's soldiers to live a life of danger on the hills. All Margaret wants is to make Jesus Christ the most important person in the church and in her life ... but will this conviction cost Margaret her life?

William Tyndale has enemies at every turn - even the King of England. Will he manage to get the Bible translated into the English language or will the priests and the royal household put a stop to him?

Both Margaret and William had to suffer for their faith and both paid the ultimate price with their lives - but they and others like them tell us that the truth is worth living for and dying for.

Special features:
Discussion starters, Bible Studies and 1600's timeline.

Danger on the Hill
The true story of Margaret Wilson by Catherine Mackenzie
ISBN:1-85792-784-2
The Smuggler's Flame
The true story of William Tyndale by Lori Rich
ISBN: 1-85792-972-1

Start collecting the Lightkeepers series now!

Ten Boys who Changed the World

By Irene Howat

David Livingstone, Billy Graham, Brother Andrew, John Newton, William Carey, George Müller, Nicky Cruz, Eric Liddell, Luis Palau, Adoniram Judson.

ISBN1 85792 5793

Ten Girls who Changed the World

By Irene Howat

Corrie Ten Boom, Mary Slessor, Joni Eareckson Tada, Isobel Kuhn, Amy Carmichael, Elizabeth Fry, Evelyn Brand, Gladys Aylward, Catherine Booth, Jackie Pullinger.

ISBN1 85792 6498

Ten Boys who Made a Difference

By Irene Howat

Augustine of Hippo, Jan Hus, Martin Luther, Ulrich Zwingli, William Tyndale, Hugh Latimer, John Calvin, John Knox, Lord Shaftesbury, Thomas Chalmers.

ISBN1 85792 7753

Ten Girls who Made a Difference

By Irene Howat

Monica of Thagaste, Catherine Luther, Susanna Wesley, Ann Judson, Maria Taylor, Susannah Spurgeon, Bethan Lloyd-Jones, Edith Schaeffer, Sabina Wurmbrand, Ruth Bell Graham.

ISBN1 85792 7761

Ten Boys who Made History

By Irene Howat

Charles Spurgeon, Jonathan Edwards, Samuel Rutherford, D L Moody, Martin Lloyd Jones, A W Tozer, John Owen, Robert Murray McCheyne, Billy Sunday, George Whitfield.

ISBN1 85792 8369

Ten Girls who Made History

By Irene Howat

Ida Scudder, Betty Green, Jeanette Li, Mary Jane Kinnaird, Bessie Adams, Emma Dryer, Lottie Moon, Florence Nightingale, Heanrietta Mears, Elisabeth Elliot.

ISBN1 85792 8377

Ten Boys who Didn't Give In

By Irene Howat

Polycarp, Alban, Sir John Oldcastle' Thomas Cranmer, George Wishart, James Chalmers, Dietrich, Bonhoeffer, Nate Saint, Ivan Moiseyev, Graham Staines.

ISBN 1 84550 0350

Ten Girls who Didn't Give In

By Irene Howat

Belina, Perpetua, Lady Jane Grey, Anne Askew, Lysken Dirks, Marion Harvey, Margaret Wilson, Judith Weinberg, Betty Stam, Esther John.

ISBN 1 84550 0369

John Welch: The Man who couldn't be Stopped

By Ethel Barrett

Find out how one of Scotland's most adventurous preachers conquered ruffians, saved a town from the dreaded plague and even dodged a cannon ball!

ISBN 1 85792 9284

Wilfred Grenfell: The Arctic Adventurer

By Linda Finlayson

Take part in the adventure that is the life of Dr Wilfred Grenfell, missionary and medic to the frozen wastelands of Labrador and Newfoundland.

ISBN 1 85792 9292

Staying faithful - Reaching out!

Christian Focus Publications publishes books for adults and children under its three main imprints: Christian Focus, Mentor and Christian Heritage. Our books reflect that God's word is reliable and Jesus is the way to know him, and live for ever with him.

Our children's publication list includes a Sunday school curriculum that covers pre-school to early teens; puzzle and activity books. We also publish personal and family devotional titles, biographies and inspirational stories that children will love.

If you are looking for quality Bible teaching for children then we have an excellent range of Bible story and age specific theological books.

From pre-school to teenage fiction, we have it covered!